HEALING AND REGENERATION THROUGH COLOR

By
CORINNE HELINE

A companion study to
Healing and Regeneration Through Music
by the same author

DeVorss and Company, *Publishers*
P.O. Box 550
Marina del Rey, CA 90291

Seventeenth Edition, 1980

ISBN: 0-87516-430-7

Printed in United States of America by
Book Graphics, Inc., Marina del Rey, CA 90291

Healing and Regeneration Through Color

IN THIS VOLUME

The Mystery of Color
The Holy Ghost Manifest in Tone and Color
The Twelve Signs and the Seven Planets
in Chromotherapy
Color Symbology of the Signs and Planets
in Relation to Jewels
Stellar Hieroglyphics in the Plant World
Flowers and the Mystery of Color
Music and Color
Color and Human Expression
Color Therapeutics
Occult Principles Emphasized in Color Therapeutics
New Age Color-Music
Color and the Regenerative Process
The Protective Aura
Color Values in Character Building
Supernatural Powers in Color
Color and the Four Sacred Seasons
Spiritual Significance of the Spectrum
Black and White

THE MYSTERY OF COLOR

Rhythmic motion is the second syllable of the Creative Word; the first is Light and the third is Color.

LIGHT is the positive or masculine force in nature; color is its negative or feminine force. Colors are light at varying rates of vibration and are produced by the differentiation of primal light as it passes through the ethers. Pure polarized ether is the only substance which is entirely colorless. Matter has been called "bottled up light" and science now declares that light possesses atomicity in addition to its wave-like attributes.

Sunlight has seven major colors visible to normal human vision and has been found to possess in addition two colorless rays, one below red and one above violet. Beyond the ultra-violet science has discovered a so-called "black field" in which are colors of a higher and rarer luminosity, a fact serving to bring the teaching of academic sciences considerably closer to that of spiritual science.

While light vibrates, it also travels at the rate of 186,000 miles per second, producing waves measuring three one-hundred-thousandths of an inch in the case of red light and one-half that for violet. Below thirty-two impulses per second vibration is inaudible as well as invisible; above that, vibration is heard as a note of music.

When light is passed through a prism, its seven rays become visible in a band called the spectrum, which contains the whole gamut of colors from red to violet. Nature's most familiar and gorgeous demonstration of this spectrum is the rainbow.

The most stupendous of earthly color spectacles are the great polar lights, the aurora borealis and aurora australis. These are magnificent outpourings of varicolored light. To the material scientists they are vast fields of magnetic effulgence; but to the occult investigator they are auric emanations of the Christ Spirit which annually penetrate and encircle the earth. The auroral vibrations are gradually absorbed by the auric envelopes of the earth and tend to refine and spiritualize the planet and beings that dwell upon it. They become visible only at the poles because the polar areas are virtually devoid of living creatures. Inhabited areas absorb this force so completely that none remains visible to the human eye. When the spiritual aspect of this sublime phenomenon is understood, one beholds its majesty with deep and reverential awe.

Esoteric interpretation is now beginning to find its verification in the discoveries of modern science. Mr. R. A. Madill, a Canadian astronomer, after extensive and intensive research, is able to confirm the long-doubted idea that the northern lights at times penetrate the atmosphere and reach the surface of the earth. The following is quoted from a newspaper interview:

Mr. Madill describes the experience of one of his friends who found himself bathed in the weird auroral lights one night. This was far up in the Arctic Circle at an outpost mission.

One of the mission buildings a few hundred feet away from where he stood became illuminated and appeared to be dissolving upward in a great elongated pillar of light. The observer then found himself within the circle of electrification and felt a flow of exhilaration. His body, he said, felt stirred and stimulated as if he had made contact with a vivifying electric current. But the moment he had passed out of the glow there was a sensation of suddenly turned off vitality. This exhilarating effect of the rays of the "northern lights" seems to be an accepted fact among the natives in the Far North, Mr. Madill reported. On nights when the display of the aurora was particularly vigorous, the people found their senses too keyed up to go to sleep.

"We are convinced that aurora borealis is a phenomenon allied to the earth's magnetism," says Mr. Madill. "The fact that the zone of greatest auroral frequency comes very near the north magnetic pole of the earth is a significant fact. In this region of greatest display of the 'northern lights' there occurs every known variety of magnetic and electric disturbances, both internal and external.

"We are fairly sure now that the aurora is caused by an invisible energy from the sun," the astronomer explained, "maybe ultraviolet rays which affect the rarefied gases of the upper

atmosphere."

Mr. Madill concludes: "If only the spectacle were commoner in inhabited regions, instead of being confined mostly to the bleak Arctic and Antarctic, the beauties of the aurora would be sung by poets even more than those of sunrises or sunsets."

Not only can white light reveal colors to outer and inner vision, but it also releases tone upon inward hearing. Science is now perfecting a means by which the *sound* of color is made audible. The mystery of color-hearing is the subject of a treatise which appeared some time ago in Paris and aroused much interest on the Continent among both scientists and artists. After the publication of this study, other scientists became interested and attempted to work out, in harmony with Newtonian physics, a complete coordination between sight and sound. Since this work was purely scientific, artistic values were ignored. To bring out these values artists have investigated the subject on their own behalf and have made contributions of a subjective nature based on findings arrived at primarily through intuition.

The spiritual scientist views with intense interest the investigations and deductions of both groups, realizing that each is approaching the central Truth by a different avenue and that eventually the two will resolve their apparent differences through an acceptance of facts already known to the occultist. Not until then will either group find a full and satisfying answer to its investigations, for complete and comprehensive knowledge of the blending of color and tone, and their spiritual relationship, can be obtained only through spiritual perception, since this involves mysteries belonging to higher planes wherein the physical senses do not function.

That this development for humanity in general is not far off is shown in the widespread interest aroused by these investigations, such interest being in itself a sign of spiritual awakening, which always bears fruit in an extension of human powers. Those who are interested in etheric colors are just touching the borderline of a new world. Vast and far-reaching in its effects is this Wonderland. Colors are to play a most important part in the evolution of humanity. Through the education of children, in anatomical and psychological research, in the diagnosis and healing of disease, in the interpretation of music and the perfecting of flowers, to name but a few developments, we are to learn something of the divinity of color.

Says Jacob Bonggren, L.D.: "Color is life—Life is Color, the vibrating, vitalic, vitaminic energy manifest in all animal, mineral and vegetable nature."

The Pittsburgh Plate Glass Company of Tampa, Florida, issued with their compliments an illustrated booklet on *Color Dynamics for the House*. The following is quoted from its introductory article, entitled *Utilize the Energy of Color:*

Laboratory tests and practical experience prove that there is Energy in Color *which affects your health, comfort, happiness and safety. By using the* Energy in Color *you can paint yourself a home not only lovely to look at, but also lovely to live in.*

When our color engineers started their study of the use of color in industry, educational institutions, office buildings, stores and homes, they were determined to explore the physiological and psychological reactions and benefits that occur in these various fields of operation.

Their conclusions were that these things are due to the Energy in Color. *Color, in the form of light, is part of the electro-magnetic spectrum. Light is one of its many octaves; others are cosmic rays, gamma rays, X-rays, ultra-violet rays, infra-red rays, radio and television rays—all possessing energy, yes, all,* including light, *possessing energy. Science has established these facts:*

1. *All electro-magnetic waves are identical except in wave length and frequency.*
2. *All types of radiant energy travel at the same rate of speed— 186,000 miles per second, and this, divided by the wave length of each, establishes its frequency.*
3. *Each color has a definite wave length—from 1/16 to 1/32 millionth of an inch—and therefore varies in frequency and impact force.*
4. *The value of each hue is controlled by its amplitude, light values having greater amplitude than dark values.*
5. *The waves of the electro-magnetic spectrum serve an almost limitless number of uses—radio, television, infra-red photography, ultraviolet lamps, fluorescent lights and X-ray machines.*

Since the many types of rays in the electro-magnetic spectrum possess great energy and perform definite functions, it is factual that light rays, which are part of this spectrum, possess usable energy.

Variation in the number of impacts upon the eye affects muscular, mental and nervous activity. For example, tests show that under ordinary light, muscular activity is twenty-three empirical units. It advances slightly under blue light. Green light increases it a little more. Yellow light raises it to thirty units. Subject a person to a given color for as little as five minutes and his mental as well as his muscular activity changes.

The medical profession has long realized that colors can be used to stimulate or depress. Some help people relax and be cheerful. Others stimulate and invigorate them. Still others set up irritation and actual physical discomfort.

Originally developed to increase efficiency in industry, its use has accomplished results in scores of great plants that are truly phenomenal. Testimonials tell how this science reduces workers' eye fatigue, lifts spirits, improves quality and quantity of production. Accidents are reduced.

Its use in hospitals has speeded recovery of patients, effectiveness of medical and nursing staffs has been raised.

In schools concentration is assisted, energy stimulated, eye fatigue retarded among students and teachers alike. Leading hotels have utilized Color Dynamics to import an atmosphere of friendliness, comfort, and good cheer. Offices are made to seem more spacious, pleasing to the eye, contributing to the health and efficiency of employees.

Color Dynamics is in no way an experiment. Its principles have been widely tested in many fields with uniformly beneficial results.

THE HOLY GHOST MANIFEST
IN TONE AND COLOR

Brahma creates perpetually. Vishnu preserves eternally. Shiva destroys and transmutes unceasingly. The color of Brahma is red as Blood! Of Vishnu, blue as the heavens and the sea; and Shiva, white with the ashes of the dead who are ever burned in His Honor!

Man lives and moves and has his being in God. That this is a literal fact becomes indubitably apparent when consciousness is raised sufficiently to study the inner workings of color and tone.

The Logos embraces within Himself all things, as White Light enfolds all colors, but His emanations are threefold. His vibratory rhythm is "stepped down" into three varying degrees, which in Christian parlance are known as the powers of Father, Son and Holy Ghost. When God said, "Let there be Light," the earth-in-the-making was flooded with a new and powerful effulgence of primordial White Light. This all-pervading Light was broken up by the threefold Divine Power into three primary colors: blue, yellow and red.

In the blue ray is made manifest creative power, or God the Father. In the yellow ray is made manifest the forming and sustaining power of Christ the Son. In the red ray is made manifest the active and disintegrating power of the Holy Ghost.

Color and sound are aspects of vibration. Herein we have the secret of ancient Mystery Teachings concerning the Word, or Logos, which, by intoning the "harmony of the spheres," causes pure color to be made manifest. Thus, the seven colors of the spectrum are attuned to the seven tones of the musical scale. The three primary colors compose the first chord in music: red is the color responding to the vibration of the key of C; yellow vibrates to E; blue to G—the first, third, and fifth intervals of which this musical chord is composed. The same triple rhythm has been discovered in the rays of the spectrum. To quote Hargarve Jennings in *The Mysteries of the Rosicrucians:* "The chemical rays, typified by the Egyptians under the name of their divinity, Thoth, are most powerful in the morning; the luminous rays (Isis) are most active at noon. The heating rays (Osiris) are most operative in the afternoon. The chemical rays are the most powerful in the spring (germination), the luminous in summer (ripening), the heating in autumn (perpetuating)."

Rays from the Sun, the planets and the Moon as they play upon the earth are also tritoned and tricolored. The blue ray in G causes germination. The yellow ray responding to E produces nutrition. The red ray responding to C is active in producing growth and the disintegration of forms when they have served their purpose.

The threefold power also operates directly in furthering the growth and development of man physically, mentally and spiritually.

The blue ray is assimilated by the spiritual center in the head and awakens within man a knowledge of his own inherent divinity. The yellow ray stimulates mental growth by way of the brain. The red ray furnishes sustenance for the physical body, gaining entrance by way of the breath.

The two powerful head centers, the pineal and pituitary glands, under the influence of Neptune and Uranus respectively, become, when awakened, the signatures of the citizen of the New Age. Uranus opens the etheric doors between heaven and earth, whereby an ever increasing number on either side of the veil are able to greet each other in the exultant realization that there is no death. Neptune enables one so illumined to enter the heavenly realms and study at first-hand the laws and so-called miracles of life pertaining to the higher planes. The accelerated vibrations necessary to awaken the power centers of the pineal and pituitary glands from latency into activity will, in many instances, be accomplished through color stimulation, thereby causing such persons to become here and now citizens of "two worlds" or "rovers amid the stars," as such attainment was designated by the early Wisdom Sons of Egypt.

The color radiations of the pineal gland, after it has begun to function spiritually, is an exquisite blue-lavendar which grows softer and more luminous with higher aspirational living. The pituitary gland emits a clear blue radiance that is tinged with golden light. The thyroid or throat center, the soft green of early spring, spangled with gold. The colors radiating from the four other principal power centers of the body are the deep and powerful golden pulsations from the heart, golden-pink from the spleen, orange from the solar-plexus and reddish-indigo at the base of the spine.

These colors are modified and varied by the spiritual and mental awareness of the person. Thus each and every personality presents a different and interesting study in color and its varied overtones. A device now perfected for transferring the gorgeous symphonies of color upon textiles and cloth will begin to revolutionize man's color consciousness and aid in the development of a sensitive and innerplane awareness which will greatly enhance the quality, tone and productiveness of all the creative arts.

The first article of wearing apparel to be so fashioned is the scarf—a significant fact since this accessory is worn about the head and throat, both of which are highly radio-magnetic and spiritual centers of man's body-temple. The throat or larynx is the focusing point of the Spoken Word. It is by means of this center that the Indwelling Spirit establishes communication with the outer objective world. Speech is man's highest attribute and the modulations of the voice are a fair index of a person's evolutionary development. This power center is as yet in the infancy of its evolvement. Its forces are governed by Mercury, the planet whose chief work with man in his present stage of development is to initiate him into the mysteries of vibration. Fourth dimensional activities will come noticeably to the fore in science, art, literature and religion. Humanity stands upon the threshold of a more colorful world which will be outstanding in its challenge to the unknown, the undiscovered and the unlimited.

The spirit, when first differentiated within the body of God or the Logos, appeared as a luminous white spark, and within this spark could be seen the glow of the three primary deific colors: blue, yellow and red. In the highest heaven world the Ego manifests as a blue light; as it descends towards physical birth it becomes on the next lower plane a yellow spark; in the third degree of its descent it takes on the vibration of red.

During the first three of the prenatal months, the Ego works in the blue flame; the fourth, fifth and sixth months, in the yellow; and the last three, in the red. Nine is the birth number and red is its color.

Thus it is that earth man receives the influence of the three primaries, or the Holy Trinity in tone and color. These primary divisions are applicable to the human race in its entirety.

Goethe, the noted German seer and poet, gave perhaps the most beautiful mystic definition of color when he stated that *colors are the sufferings of light.* In other words, the Logos "steps down" the vibrations of the White Light so that they can better serve the needs of our planetary evolution.

Sacrifice is the keynote of all progression in every round of life from the atom to God. The White Light, containing all colors within itself, lowers its vibratory rate (sacrifices itself) to produce the spectrum.

The Zodiac lowers its vibrations (sacrifices itself) for the sake of our planetary system.

It was in 1692 that Isaac Newton announced his discovery of the fact that sunlight can be broken up into varying colors of different degrees of frangibility which comprise the seven colors of the solar spectrum. But there is little doubt that this was also part of the Wisdom Teachings of the ancients as shown particularly in the sacred stepped pyramids of Chaldea. Much knowledge was lost with the disappearance of the Mystery Temples in their outward form.

The seven colors are capable of still further division in that each color runs the gamut of seven degrees in an increasing refinement of shade derived from its particular color note.

When the scale of color is completed in violet, another octave begins, with twice the number of vibrations of the lower scale. The radiant, living beauty of these etheric colors is beyond description. As man learns to project his sight into inner planes he will find himelf in possession of a new spectrum. The glory of our rainbow is but a faint reflection of this.

THE TWELVE SIGNS AND SEVEN PLANETS IN CHROMOTHERAPY

H. P. Blavatsky asserts that yellow radiations strengthen the right eye and indigo radiations the left eye. This information, she states, started her pupils on a search which ended in the discovery of occult chromotherapy.

The colors of the twelve signs are transmitted to earth by means of the Sun as the central reflector and by the other planets of the solar system.

Emanations of the twelve zodiacal Hierarchies (signs) play upon the body of man, each having its own special or psychic entrance gate. The human organism is a sounding board for each zodiacal body emitting its own particular keynote and raying forth its own syncronous color.

In conformity with the starry pattern above in which the twelve signs are divisible into a quartenary corresponding with the four elements—Fire, Air, Earth and Water—so also there are the four principal differentiations in the vehicles which man uses in his progressive evolution.

The Fire signs, Aries, Leo and Sagittarius, represent the pure flame of Spirit. The Air signs, Gemini, Libra and Aquarius, typify the powers of mind. The Water signs, Cancer, Scorpio and Pisces, the emotional nature. The Earth signs, Taurus, Virgo and Capricorn, the physical or human body-temple.

Each of the twelve signs emits its own individual sound and radiates its own individual color. Each tone has its seven octaves and each color possesses its seven varying color notes. Some of these color notes are too delicate to be sensed as yet by the physical eye, but already their effect upon body and consciousness are beginning to be tabulated in color psychology and color therapeutics. In proportion to these enlarging discoveries will color come into its own as a remedial agent to be used for the healing of

Healing and Regeneration through Color

various inharmonies connected with the physical, emotional, mental and spiritual life of man.

The twelve zodiacal signs bestow vitality of varying degrees as well as different characteristics, temperament and personal appearance. They are truly signposts of life, and the response or affinity of each individual spirit to the varying degrees of tone and color, as emanated by the birth sign, indicates the native's evolutionary status. This fact also aids adaptability or susceptibility of healing through music and color.

Light is reflected upon the earth in a sevenfold ray and there are seven spirits before the throne of God—the planets belonging to our solar system, each of which is a messenger for one of the seven rays.

In accordance with its own spiritual development, each planet receives its color ray from the Sun. Saturn receives and disseminates one of the highest vibrations of the sevenfold spectrum, hence its color-tone is termed indigo. Jupiter, the royal planet, sends forth purple rays of stately beneficence; Mars, the martial star, the fiery color of red; Venus, the illumining and inspiring tones of yellow; the Sun, the health promoting orange ray. Earth reflects the soothing and healing green of her nature tones; Uranus, the mystic and electric blue; Neptune, the lavendars and orchids belonging particularly to the New Age. Mercury is the messenger and reflector of the sevenfold ray in synthesis by virtue of its close proximity to the Sun, and from the Sun receives its fundamental impress of deep yellow with overtones of violet.

Although not belonging to this particular solar system (from an occult standpoint), Neptune is included because its rays are of interest in a treatise on color. The Sun color is also given although the Sun is not a planet and we ordinarily consider its "color" to be white, or the synthesis of colors analyzed in the solar spectrum. Esoterically, however, the Sun itself is but the center of focus of the invisible Light of the Logos for our planetary system, and has a basic color of its own: orange, the color taken by esotericists in meditation upon the Sun and in using the solar forces for purposes of healing.

Pluto, another recent visitor within the limits of astronomical observation, emits an electric red, lightning-like ray. Pluto is considered to be the higher octave of Mars and its rulership is ascribed to the constellation Scorpio.

The physical body of man is a musical instrument which is either in tune with celestial harmonies or in dissonance with them according to the degree of health, well-being and advancement of the individual. This glorious instrument of the Spirit becomes a center of scintillating and radiant color as the forces of the twelve starry Hierarchies and of their seven planetary Messengers play upon it.

When parents and teachers become wise enough to substitute these heavenly values in both color and tone for the dull fabrics and blatant jazz now so prevalent in nurseries, kindergartens and schools, a new world education will have begun. The average child will be transformed into a precocious one. Problems of delinquency will diminish and a wiser, more responsible-minded generation will take possession of the earth.

The Moon, through its green ray, controls and maintains the glandular system; the Sun, by its orange ray, the heart and sympathetic nervous system; Mercury projects its mixed yellow-violet effusions upon the lungs, cerebro-spinal nerves and, in particular, upon the right cerebral brain hemisphere. The yellow beam of Venus plays upon the skin of the entire body and affects particularly the kidneys. The red forces of Mars tinge the whole muscular organism and control the left cerebral brain hemisphere. The royal purple of Jupiter influences the entire circulatory system; the indigo powers of Saturn, the complete bony structure.

The soft electric blue of Uranus stimulates the ductless glands in general and accelerates certain dormant but powerful body centers. The lavender and orchid shades of Neptune arouse the sleeping spinal fire and tend to blend harmoniously the etheric currents of the two great nerve systems, the sympathetic and the cerebro-spinal.

Thus, through color and tone the Starry Lords of heaven are transforming matter into spirit and mortality into glorious immortality.

COLOR SYMBOLOGY OF THE SIGNS AND PLANETS IN RELATION TO JEWELS

There is a philosophy of color in relation to minerals which has come down to us from antiquity, based upon the fact that the twelve zodiacal Hierarchies who work with the mineral kingdom infuse into its component parts something of the force and rhythm which belong to themselves. All minerals and gems are, therefore, attuned to some one of the twelve constellations and proclaim this affinity by their color.

By virtue of this fact anyone possessing or wearing metals or jewels attracts to himself the planetary forces to which they are related.

The ancients held that every gem was originally crystallized by and around an entity which had a real, though subjective (or inner plane), activity and awareness. This entity was capable of impressing the subconscious mind of the person possessing the gem as to coming events, thereby enabling him to avoid danger or to embrace opportunities. Hence, the great importance of wearing jewels in harmony with one's stellar rays.

Ancients who understood and made use of these hidden and now well-nigh forgotten powers existent in jewels, fashioned talismans which were magnets of great potency, either for good or evil in accordance with their use. They were capable of transmitting powers making for the restoration of health and well-being, and equally able to convey forces carrying in their train destruction and death. Silversmiths, goldsmiths and lapidaries of early times ranked with apothecaries as skilled magicians.

The records of early Christian writers reveal a belief that the stones in the Breastplate of the High Priest were so highly magnetized by their respective planetary rulers that they were capable of responding to questions in flashing color language. It is known also that Hermetic Brotherhood strictly observed rules relating to the use of precious stones on days corresponding to their planetary affinities, knowing well the powers of such association.

The correlation of jewels to the days of the week are as follows:

Sunday	Sun's day	Gold and Yellow gems.
Monday	Moon's day	Pearls and all white stones.
Tuesday	Mars' day	Rubies and all red stones.
Wednesday	Mercury's day	Turquoise (to claim protection from the Air with whom Mercury is closely allied), Sapphire and blue stones.
Thursday	Jupiter's day	Amethyst, and purple stones.
Friday	Venus' day	Emerald and green stones.
Saturday	Saturn's day	Diamond; also black stones.

The generally accepted correlation of metals and precious stones with their zodiacal focii and color is as follows:

Sign	Jewels	Metal	Color
Aries	Ruby, Bloodstone, Red Jasper	Iron	Red
Taurus	Golden Topaz, Coral, Emerald	Copper	Yellow
Gemini	Crystal, Carbuncle, Aquamarine	Mercury	Violet
Cancer	Emerald, Moonstone	Silver	Green
Leo	Ruby, Sardonyx, Amber	Gold	Orange
Virgo	Pink Jasper, Turquoise, Zircon	Mercury	Violet
Libra	Opal, Diamond	Copper	Yellow
Scorpio	Agate, Garnet, Topaz	Iron	Red
Sagittarius	Amethyst	Tin	Purple
Capricorn	Black-and-white Onyx, Beryl, Jet	Lead	Blue
Aquarius	Blue Sapphire	Lead	Indigo
Pisces	Diamond, Jade	Tin	Indigo

STELLAR HIEROGLYPHICS IN THE PLANT WORLD

FOOD IN RELATION TO COLOR

Color sounds the command of the Future. Everything black, grey and misty has already sufficiently submerged the consciousness of humanity. One must again ponder about the gorgeous flower colours which always heralded the epochs of renaissance. —Nicholas Roerich.

When the Sun enters Aries at the Spring Equinox, the earth is bathed in the fires of a new year. The color of Aries is red, and the plants formed upon the earth by this vibration are red rhubarb, berries and all fiery greens: mustard, onions, radishes, peppers.

Natives under Aries and any of the other fire signs should choose a diet largely from foods growing above ground.

The color of Taurus is yellow and its plants are mostly yellow. Many of the familiar garden vegetables belong to this sign such as yellow beets, beans, sweet potatoes and carrots.

Earth signs harmonize with foods growing beneath or in the earth. Natives coming under the earth and water signs need the earth forces as much as the fire and air signs require the powers of the Sun.

Gemini color is violet. Prolific bearers in the vegetable kingdom belong to this sign. Also green vegetables and acid fruits. People belonging to the air signs need foods grown above ground, but not to the same extent as do the fire signs. They also require a more varied diet.

The colors of Cancer are white and green. Cancer plants are cucumbers, squash and all kinds of melons. Cancer natives respond to the fruits and greens that grow in the shade and are reached only by indirect sunlight.

Leo with his orange ray requires for its natives' well-being that they draw especially on the yellow foods richest in the life vitamins formed by the direct Sun rays. Yellow foods are richest in vitamin C content.

Virgo's colors are violet and gold. The golden russet foods of autumn give health and sustenance to its own. All grains, as barley, oats, rye and wheat, form under the Virgo Ray.

To Libra belongs the autumn glory of golden yellow and crimson. Librans respond particularly to the red and yellow fruits and to all vegetables grown above ground.

The reds and deep scarlets of the martial ray are Scorpio's. Its best foods are red and yellow. The water triplicity, particularly Scorpio, should partake freely of watery fruits and vegetables.

The color of Sagittarius is royal purple, and the best foods for this regal fire sign are those which are tinged with the crimson and gold of the Sun's direct power.

Fire signs can assimilate raw foods more easily than the other three triplicities.

Capricorn's colors are indigo and black-and-white. All foods grown in the earth are most easily assimilated in the Capricornian's regular diet. The native of this sign may partake without harmful effects of richer foods than any of the other earthy signs. The earth signs require more food than either the fire, air or water, and also may partake regularly of a richer diet.

The colors of Aquarius are indigo and white. The foods are largely the white fruits and vegetables. Celery, asparagus, parsnips, potatoes and pears are especially good. All air signs can partake freely of all white, starchy vegetables. Aquarius requires less food than any of the other twelve signs.

The Piscean colors are silvery blue and sea green. The foods best assimilated are warm tropical fruits and vegetables such as dates, pomegranites, white figs; also all vegetables grown below ground.

Earth signs require a regular and substantial diet.

Air signs require much lighter food and a larger variety.

Fire signs require a larger protein content in diet.

Water signs require lighter food and a goodly amount of nourishing liquids.

(The above is not intended as a complete diet list, but only to note certain foods most easily assimilated by natives of the different signs in relation to color harmonies.)

The following suggests something of the psychological effect of color in connection with food:

From an unidentified press clipping: "Peach color arouses hunger. The color has been proven to be the most 'appetizing' hue for eating places in tests conducted by cafeterias and restaurants. Other wall colors which are also effective are turquoise blue, light coral and bright yellow." Another press clipping, with a New York date line, quotes the report of an industrial designer and color consultant who conducted experiments in restaurants. "Color has a powerful influence on the subconscious. . . . For instance there was a cafeteria chain which wanted to improve its salad sales and did so by replacing the usual white crockery with pale green plates. The sales went up over 100 percent." He also tells of a fruit dealer painting the walls of his store a bright orange. "This orange color made the produce look appetizing," said the expert, "tying in nicely with the colors of fruits and vegetables. . . . Sales boomed!" And on railroad dining cars: "The blue fluorescent lighting made the coffee look weak and gray, and the diners didn't like it. They were tasting coffee with their eyesight!"

The subject of color in connection with food offers a wide field for experimentation. It holds one of the keys to physical health, so let us look forward to the day when the therapeutic values of color vibration come into their own.

FLOWERS AND THE MYSTERY OF COLOR

Earth's crammed with heaven,
And every common bush afire with God,
But only he who sees takes off his shoes.
—Elizabeth Barrett Browning.

Paracelsus tells us that if we knew all the qualities of the stars we would find that the "quality of each one of them is represented on earth by some plants. It is no inconsistent thing to say that every stone, flower and tree has its horoscope."

The Group Spirit of plants, from its focus in the center of the earth, also emanates a spectrum of light which is absorbed by the roots of plants, carried up in the life force or sap, and used by nature spirits to color the plant kingdom exactly in accordance with its varying development. Thus, flowers truly "write music in the air," proclaiming to all who observe them the position of their evolutionary status. White roses represent the highest stage of progress. Their perfume is generally the most delicate because the human sense of smell is as yet too unrefined to receive its full vibratory emanation.

Blue flowers are next in development. They are not only more rare but much more fragile. The yellow follows; then the pink; lowest in color rate and most hardy in physical endurance are the reds.

From an unidentified newspaper clipping we quote:

There are some indications that in pre-historic times, before the Carboniferous Period, the earth was comparatively devoid of color. Some enthusiasts even see in the development of the color sense a result of the "survival of the fittest." The appreciation of color in the aesthetic sense is certainly a product of cultural advancement. Children and savages love bright and garish colors;

Healing and Regeneration through Color

culture and refinement (if not decadence) make for a liking of the soft, subdued tints.

The above recent findings of modern science are in complete harmony with spiritual science. The Carboniferous Period of the former is the Lemurian Epoch of the latter. As man evolves he touches new gradations of color. There were few flowers in Lemuria; mostly dense green forests and heavy tropical vegetation. The color green is due for tremendous development. It is the earth color, and future Burbanks will produce beautiful green flowers when man learns to use this color as the wonderful curative agency it is destined to become.

The early Atlanteans knew flowers but not the delicate, dainty hues of today. Theirs were heavy brick reds, russet browns and purplish blacks. When the nadir of materiality had been reached and man turned heavenward once more, the Christed vibration, which is centered within the earth, opened the way for pastel tints to develop in greater beauty and variety as the earth and man became increasingly attuned to it.

As the Cosmic Christ Principle awakens increasingly the Christ principle in man, altruism, compassion and selfless serving will be correspondingly evidenced in the world. A direct manifestation of this fact will be found in pastel tints objectified in the realm of color. Delicate blues are still rare and fragile in the flower world because the operation of pure spiritual impulse is so rare in humankind.

As previously stated, there are seven gradations to each of the seven colors of the spectrum. Later, these will be extended to twelve, and the physical solar spectrum now known to science will also be enlarged to include twelve color-tones. The color scale of seven tones will be augmented to respond to th twelve-toned chromatic scale.

The more of the Light and Reflecting Ethers (the two highest of the four ethers) which man attracts to himself through high and inspirational living, the more of the beautiful he will find surrounding him. Truly as the poet has said: "Beauty is in the eye of the beholder."

Certain vibratory rates manifest to physical perception as color. This color vibration is drawn from the Sun by one of the seven planetary rays using the Light Ethers as the medium of transmission.

Each flowering plant produces its own "paint pot," so to speak, from which nature spirits draw the colors they use to tint petals. Annie Besant charmingly described these same little devas or nature spirits as "building in a language that is color and a motion that is melody."

Flowers also emit their fragrance in music. As with tone and color, so also many perfumes are too refined to make an impress upon the physical senses. Organs of smell, sight and hearing are due for a remarkable process of sensitization.

Many composers have caught in the strains of their flower music the perfume of the flower, a notable example being MacDowell's *To a Wild Rose*. The composer duplicated the exact pattern of melody upon which the wild rose is fashioned. If the performer is in a sensitive mood while playing this lovely music, he will discover that the atmosphere surrounding him is suffused with delicate fragrance as of attar of roses.

Fragrance is produced by the dissemination of minute particles of the flowering plant, their essential oil. Different colors are found to have different odors. Red roses emit a heavy rich perfume like deep bass notes. Pink roses shed a finer perfume which may be compared to a rich baritone. Yellow roses give out a lighter, pungent odor which may be likened to the golden notes of clear tenor or pure contralto voice. Blue is the soprano color-tone. But a white rose gives forth a high delicate fragrancy, frequently barely perceptible and comparable only to the flute-like tones of the most beautiful coloratura.

Kepler assigns to Saturn and Jupiter the bass; to Mars the tenor; to Venus and Earth the contralto; to Mercury the treble. As Hargrave Jennings well observes, "Music is always in the air, particularly at night, for nature (being born of it) is necessarily more sensitive at night to the beautiful."

Nature always works in harmony with the chromatic color scale. It has been discovered by horticulturists that when flowers are placed under blue light they grow more rapidly. Under yellow light they blossom more profusely, and under red light they have a tendency to turn back into the earth.

Dr. Enoch Karrer (Smithsonian Institute) reports:

Healing and Regeneration through Color

"Different Colors of Light cause seedling tips of plants to seek or shun each other." [Dr. Karrer grew seedlings and exposed them to the rainbow band of light obtained by splitting the white light of an electric arc.] "Blue light caused the seedlings to bend toward the light and toward each other. Red illuminated seedling tips bent away from each other. Plants receiving orange light became greener than their neighbors and roots grew longest in the extreme blue rays."

The variegated colors of a garden hold much for scientific study and spiritual meditation by every reverent observer of the deeper mysteries of life and being. Warmly will they echo the poet's utterance:

The simplest flower that grows bears throughts that lie too deep for tears.

The following is a listing of the flowers and perfrumes ascribed to the Twelve Zodiacal Signs:

Signs	*Flowers*	*Perfumes*
Aries	All small red flowers.	Red Carnation and Red Rose
Taurus	All flowers.	All Rose perfumes
Gemini	All double flowers	Lilac, Old Lavender
Cancer	Lotus and Immortelles	All Lily perfumes, Jasmine
Leo	All Golden and deep yellow flowers	Orange Blossom
Virgo	All flowers of Lily family	White Rose and Heliotrope
Libra	All Balms, Pansy, Violet, Primrose	Rosemary and Sandalwood
Scorpio	Chrysanthemum; all large red flowers	All red flower perfumes
Sagittarius	All climbing vines and flowering trees	Violet

Capricorn	All black and dark-hued flowers—blooming Cereus, Black Poppy, Nightshade.	Black Narcissus and Black Tulip
Aquarius	Blue and white flowers, Acacia, Frankincense and Myrrh.	Gardenia
Pisces	White and orchid flowers: all sea plants, Ferns and Mosses	White Narcissus

MUSIC AND COLOR

Every composer has his dominant color tone and upon that he builds the various compositions which manifest in a harmony of color as well as sound.

Every musician and every musical composition has its own fundamental color tone. That of Bach is the blue-gold of a gas flame; Beethoven's is royal purple; Tschaikowsky's is amber gold; Debussey's, clear jade; Greig's, delicate orchid; Mendelssohn's, rose pink; Schubert's, rose-lavender. Referring to his own compositions Schubert writes: "My musical productions came into existence through understanding and pain. Those which pain has brought forth seem to please the world most."

Robert Schumann's color-note is deep pink with a golden hue; Richard Wagner's pale mauve interspersed with delicate green-gold lights. The Grail music in both *Lohengrin* and *Parsifal* shimmers in tones of pure white which take the form of multitudinous miniature crosses and glow with a luminosity borrowed from heaven. Chopin's note is a mystic blue. This color-tone of Chopin's inspiration is identical with that of Lafcadio Hearn, a writer whose exquisite and magical power of tonal beauty in the use of the English langauge is unsurpassed. Hearn writes of the luminous blue tone in which he takes his inspirational flights in these words:

Even as though the jewel-radiance of the tropic stream pass undulation from the vaster deep, with their sobbings and whisperings, their fugitive drift and foam, so through emotions evolved by the vision of luminous blue there may somehow quiver back to us out of the infinite (multitudinous like the billion ether shiverings that make the blue sensation of a moment) something of all the aspirations of the ancient faiths, and the power of the vanished gods, and the passion and the beauty of all the prayers ever uttered by the lips of man.

This "infinite blue," the inspirational color ray in which Chopin composed and Lafcadio Hearn wrote, is the source upon which Maxfield Parrish has drawn for his painting. It is his visualizations in magic blue which have made him one of the most popular of contemporary artists. He can speak personally of the inspiration which this particular color ray bestows.

The same divine or Uranium blue is the chief source of inspiration for Nicholas Roerich, the great Russian-American painter who is, perhaps, the supreme artistic genius of our day. His "infinite vistas" ofttimes hold the indescribable magic of this ethereal color whose spell attunes earth with heaven.

Another familiar and beloved composer of our day is Charles Wakefield Cadman. His color note is soft woodland-green, this color being predominant in all his works.

The distinguished Russian composer, Scriabin, was experimenting most interestingly with tone and its attendant color at the time of his demise in 1915. In that which he aspired to make his greatest work, *Prometheus,* he proposed to depict in music the seven days of creation with their corresponding color tones. For this performance he wished to use "a great white hall with a bare interior dome having no architectural decorations. From this dome the shimmering colors would rush downwards in torrents of light." His death prevented the fulfillment of this dream. His ideals belong to the New Age and will later be realized in a glorious consummation of the alchemical union of two great arts, color and tone.

The item which follows is quoted from the *World Theosophist,* having been written at the time of the *Prometheus* presentation by the Chicago Symphony.

Prometheus was begun at the time Scriabin was living at Brussels in 1909, but was completed in Moscow after his return to Russia.

We shall have a better understanding of Scriabin's aims in the composition of Prometheus *if we remember that the work was largely the result of the Russian master's belief in and enthusiasm for Theosophy. This is a system that sets out to include all branches of religion, philosophy and science; which makes for a more intimate relation of the human soul with God, and believes that, as the essential divinity is in man, the gradual approach to God is made by successive reembodiments or reincarnations. This ultimate consum-*

mation is what the Buddhists term "Nirvana." Dr. Eaglefield Hull wrote thus of Scriabin's Theosophical attitude to music:

> His first symphony is a Hymn to Art and joins hands with Beethoven's Ninth. His third, the Divine Poem, expresses the spirit's liberation from its earthly trammels and the consequent free expression of purified personality; while his Poem of Ecstacy voices the highest of all joys—that of creative work. He held that in the artists' incessant creative activity, his constant progression towards the ideal, the spirit alone truly lives. In Prometheus he reaches the furthest point of his ecstasy in creative energy, a point which was to have been carried astoundingly further by his proposed Mystery, in which sounds, colors, odors, and movement were to be united in expressing one fundamental idea.
>
> It should be said, too, that the Prometheus whose name was associated by Scriabin with his work is not the Prometheus, who, according to the Greek myth, stole fire from heaven, and, as a punishment, was chained to a rock, where daily an eagle devoured his liver—a myth made familiar by the tragedy of Aeschylus. Mrs. Rosa Newmarch, a close friend of the composer, stated that Scriabin's hero was one of that class of adepts symbolized at a much later date by the Greeks under the name of Prometheus. These 'Sons of the Flame of Wisdom,' who were closely allied with the purely spiritual side of man, were alone able to impart to humanity that sacred spark which expands into the blossom of human intelligence and self-consciousness.

This work of harmonizing tone and color has been interestingly furthered in some conferences on color and music held in Hamburg, Germany, some years ago under the supervision of a scientist named Dr. Anschutz. Among other things he investigated many cases of color-hearing. We quote:

> Dr. Anschutz has issued numerous pamphlets and books on his researches. He has shown that a large number of persons connect each musical tone with a tint, more or less precisely. More rarely, they perceive a world of color when they hear music. He reports as a specially interesting case of 'color-hearing' that of an organist, Dorken, blind from the age of thirteen years.
>
> This man, despite his blindness, has retained a vivid memory of colors. Each note of the scale means for him a very definite tint.

Each human voice produces a luminous vision—pleasant or otherwise; each odor has its 'photism'; every vivid sensation such as muscular fatigue, toothache, even a hot bath, produces one. Sneezing brings it on. This sensitiveness would not seem to be a manifestation of disease.

Several professors of philosophy have aided him by making inquiries in their classes. The material thus gathered proves that 'synesthesia' of 'color-hearing' is not so rare as has been thought, and not necessarily abnormal. He divides color-audition into 'analytic synopsy'—where a color is seen for each separate tone—and 'synthetic synopsy' in which colors are seen only in moving patterns, in connection with a piece of music.

Among these latter he distinguishes three types, those that while hearing such, perceive bright, shimmering colors on unstable surfaces or in moving serpentine lines; those who hearing music, and also when they hear violent sounds, see surfaces or masses slightly colored, moving slowly, detach themselves from a somber background. A third type perceives images, colorless or colored, but generally after audition, when at rest, often just before going to sleep. The same images appear after hearing the same piece, which differentiates these 'photisms' from other kinds.

The work of Dr. Anschutz is but a forerunner of many groups which will be organized to study the mysteries of color and music and to learn to use a synthesis of color and tone for healing the physical ills of man, and also to accentuate and accelerate his moral consciousness and spiritual development.

COLOR AND HUMAN EXPRESSION

The human voice, like every musical instrument, possesses its own individual color. A chorus of voices blended in the singing of an inspired work such as the *Hallelujah Chorus* is a revelation in both beauty and sound. Bassos and baritones run the gamut of color-tones belonging to the red ray. Contraltos and altos are placed in the yellow ray; while sopranos, both mezzo and lyric, are in blue from the deepest shades up through the brightest azures. In singing, color-tones of the voice are modified and interblended to a certain extent with the color-tone of the music. This color is determined by the keynote of the musical composition.

In orchestral music there is a glorious symphony of color harmonies and tone. Each instrument has its dominant color, corresponding to its keynote, which blends with the colors of the music being played. These colors affect the hearer even though he himself is unconscious of them. The low color-tones of jazz tend to lower the vibration of a person who is ill in body or mind. In nearly all soothing, restful music there is a predominance of quiet greens; such are found in most slumber songs. The soprano voice is especially beneficial in cases of acute melancholia because it brings to the patient the blue ray from the world of pure Spirit where all is harmony and love. There are marvelous discoveries just ahead along these lines to be used for the inestimable benefit of humanity. Already colors are being experimented with in community singing to note the psychological effect upont he singers.

A famous woman pianist, in a most interesting article written for the *Musical Courier* says: "Rhythm can be visualized; motion, color, and sound are only interchangeable elements from a common source." She describes the colors which she feels in interpreting certain composers. In playing a certain nature opus of Beethoven she senses green; Sinding, a green-yellow; and Chopin, blue-violet. In making these experiments she comes very close to the occult when she says: "Would it not be better if we would bring ourselves to closing eyes and stilling curious index fingers and so learning to communicate with more sensitive antennae?" And she interestingly adds: "Is this not simply the spiritual rebirth which our age must come to mean after the years of intellectual vivisection that are just now coming to an end?"

One of the leading exponents of aesthetic dancing conducted a fascinating series of color experiments with his pupils, both individually and collectively. He found that grey costumes produce a listless effect on the dancers; warm reds, great activity of individual expression; rich purple and Italian blue, a most joyful effect; black was conducive to aesthetic movement but lacked spontaneity. He proclaimed this experimentation with colors to be a most delightful study and only in the beginning of its development. He is preparing to study further by experimenting with costumes of one shade and surroundings of another. He believes that color produces a greater effect upon a dancer than upon any other artist.

Students of occult arts and those mystically inclined, when utilizing any of the fine arts as mediums through which to promulgate the higher principles governing life, will find it helpful to draw upon the exquisite lavender tones belonging to Neptune. Writers and speakers whose message is centered in the New Age ideals of unity, cooperation and brotherhood will find their inspiration sharpened by the use of the clear blue of Uranus.

Teachers, scientists, physicians, nurses and metaphysical healers will be strengthened in their respective professions by using the soft, pure violet and gold of Mercury. Mothers, teachers of very young children, matrons of orphanages, and all who have the care and direction of young children, will be greatly aided and stimulated in their work by the use of the lovely soft and tender yellow tones of Venus.

The deitician, naturopath, chiropractor, osteopath and other healers following natural methods of correction and restoration, will be definitely helped in their ministrations by centering largely in the pure orange of the Sun together with the clear healing violet of Mercury.

Ministers, lawyers, public speakers and politicians will enhance their powers and influence by using the pure purple of Jupiter. Athletes, soldiers, farmers and all outdoor workers will increase both energy and endurance by use of the clean, clear reds of Mars.

The Moon influences prenatal growth and the early years of infancy. Its soft, mist-like green and silver tones are used for infantile ills and also during the months of prospective motherhood.

Spirit, mind and body, or man in the whole of his being, was atuned to the heavenly spheres. Disease would never have touched that wholeness or disturbed the harmony he once knew had he always lived true to Cosmic Law.

COLOR THERAPEUTICS

The following excerpt, expressing the views of a noted English investigator upon the subject of color as a panacea for human ills, is of genuine interest:

Colors are effective as a cure for disease and may even add ten years to the life of a human being, according to Lord Clifford of Chudleigh, who has studied the action of light shades on vegetable growth for many years.

He believes that every disease can be cured by certain colors. Yellow is the restorer of the nerves, he finds, while green increases the vitality. He says:

"One shade of red is the most effectual in all cases of blood poisoning. Ultra-violet produces a fermentation in the body which reduces hardness of tissue and also builds up blood tissues.

"A particular shade of violet causes the growth of bone; an indigo produces muscular generation and strength.

"Then there is a shade of green which produces vitality and general energy of the system and also the growth of fat; yellow restores the nerves. But, of course, the greatest care must be taken that only the right shade of each color is used or opposite results may be obtained.

"The treatment would also benefit most people suffering from premature old age and mental worry produced by past illness. It could well add ten years to their lives. I do not claim that it can make people of 60 feel like 35, but it certainly can restore them to the state of activity enjoyed a dozen years before."

One of the most important phases of healing through color and tone is the awakening realization of the healer to the fact that mind and spirit are intimately connected with physical ills, and that in them lie the cause as well as the cure of the disease.

We have noted that the twelve signs of the zodiac are divided into four triplicities correlating to the four elements in nature and also that these same divisions correlate to man's lower quartenary or the threefold body, together with mind, which constitute the composite vehicle in which the Ego functions on earth. The same fourfold classification pertains to diseases, all of which fall into one or another of these four groupings.

To illustrate, infirmities caused by alcoholic excesses, fevers, high blood pressure and that most dreaded disease of all human scourges, cancer, all come under the element of Fire. All forms of insanity and drug excesses relate to the Air element. Diseases of the stomach, digestive tract, the assimilative and glandular systems come under the Water element. All abnormal growths and malformations of the body belong to the element of Earth.

It will be understood, as previously noted, that each fundamental color has its sevenfold aspect in which it blends or unites with each of the other six colors of a new age science of color therapy or color psychology. Much experimentation and observation will be required in this new science in order to determine the varying effects of the many possible color combinations.

Persons who are highly sensitized will profit most by this innovation; also children of tender years and even those yet unborn can, in their prenatal stage, be influenced by the colors affecting the life of the mother.

We could quote at great length from medical authorities who are working along these fascinating lines of research. But these pages are devoted primarily to occult investigations, and it is in this field that the study of tone and color will ultimately be perfected. Both have their origin on levels higher than physical senses can penetrate, therefore we shall pursue our study in the light of extended perceptions of sight and sound.

In *Letters on Occult Meditation* Alice Bailey writes:

. . . lights are played on the body of the disciple and effect a shaking-out process and a simultaneous stimulation of the atoms. This cannot be done till further information is given anent the Rays; when a man's ray is known, stimulation will come from the use of his own colour, a building-in will be brought about by the use of his complementary colour, and disintegration of unwanted matter will be brought about by the use of an antagonistic colour.

This knowledge will later on be communicated to the great bodies that hold custody of the Mysteries . . . Wait, for the time is not yet.

Similar fundamental conclusions have been reached as regards color-therapy by all genuine investigators from Dr. Babbitt, as recorded in his famous *Principles of Light and Color,* to the eminent Dr. George Starr White. Experimentations in color therapeutics are being tried in a number of large hospitals at the present time. Rooms have been set aside for color treatment in which the walls, ceilings and furnishings, including even the bed linen, are all of one specific color, in accordance with the malady to be treated therein.

Care must be taken in this method of treatment. It has long been known that the exclusive use of any color other than nature's own green, if continued over a long period of time, leads to insanity. From antiquity come records of color being used in penal institutions for doing away with political prisoners. The high violet radiation produces the head-in-the-clouds type of mental imbalance; red the violent type—the two extremes of the spectrum.

Edwin M. Hale, M.D., observed:

In one of the French Insane Asylums not only the blue ray but others were tried, and the effect was very interesting—when violent and maniacal patients were placed in rooms where the red ray predominated they became worse. If the patients were removed to a room where the blue ray predominated, they became calm and quiet.

One of the Government's largest hospitals for the rehabilitation of nerve-shattered men returned from service is placing in its neuropsychiatric section for decorative purposes the color patterns for the Grail music of Lohengrin. This theme is a transcription of heavenly music. It is the chorusing of angelic choirs. The spiritual scientist knows well that hospital wards and other beds of suffering are frequented by angels who bring healing and solace to the afflicted. With the introduction of their own particular rhythms in the hospital environment, may not their presence become more clearly sensed and their ministry increasingly effective? Spiritual science and *materia medica,* each from its own point of view, are largely anticipating the perfecting of techniques and the further extension of the practice of color therapeutics.

Dr. Nyls R. Finsen, a Danish physician who was awarded the Nobel Prize for medicine in 1903, demonstrated that: Effects upon the body are due to chemical, or violet and ultra-violet rays. By filtering the light of the room through red glass, he shut off the chemical rays from smallpox patients. The result was that the vesicles did not suppurate and scars and pitting were avoided.

In the June, '48 issue of *Your Mind,* was an article by W. R. Hunt entitled "New Possibilities for Energizing Feeble Minds." It reported on work done by Mr. and Mrs. E. A. Boos in the Boos School, Plano, Ill. Color, music and pictures are combined to release the mental processes in children who are not just "backward" but those classed as idiots and imbeciles, the so-called "hopeless" ones. It is a remarkable enterprise and points the way, psychiatrically, to techniques that penetrate beyond the mind to the child's subconscious and superconscious minds. Color and music become part of the magic equipment in this most important work of bringing undeveloped minds into a state of normalcy. Occultists will be especially interested in Mr. Hunt's interpretation of the processes involved in this truly New Age therapy.

A color therapy program is being worked out in a veteran's hospital in Oakland, California. Hospital rooms with interchangeable wall coverings are giving color relief to patients. Soothing combinations of soft green, blue, peach and "sunny" yellow have replaced the deadly monotony of white walls for the veterans.

The hospital staff fitted out a twenty-three-room ward with chintz drapes made to be easily movable from one room to another. The cornice boards were painted blending colors to harmonize with the various drape colors.

So now the veteran in his bed can see a "new" room every week.

OCCULT PRINCIPLES EMPHASIZED IN COLOR THERAPEUTICS

Although scientific investigators have been able to do much in color therapy by observation of the patient's reactions to color treatments, thorough diagnosis requires the powers of extended vision whereby the patient's aura may be examined and the lack of a specific color accurately noted. The diagnosis having been made, if the sufferer does not understand the power of thought, he will be placed in a room in which the needed color predominates, all the appointments being in this hue—walls, bedding and so on. He will be told to concentrate intently upon this color in order that his imagination may be filled with it, and a strong visual image be retained. If he comprehends something of the nature of concentration and visualization, his thought alone, without external aid, is all that is necessary.

The occult student should be able to do much for himself through color visualization. "Bathing in color" is not mere fancy, but fact. Regular periods of daily meditation in which the affected organs are flooded with the color necessary for their re-invigoration will be found to be most beneficial, both from a physical standpoint and in the cultivation of powers of concentration and visualization.

The envelope of Life Spirit (universal life) which encircles the earth, bears the healing yellow ray of the Christ. Immersing the physical body in a bath of this Christ ray is most efficacious in healing maladies of mind and body. This ray was not used until the Christian Era and has, therefore, been termed the color of spiritual illumination. Yellow and blue are the colors most in use for treating the insane.

Further discoveries connected with that sphinx-like system of the body, the ductless glands, will prove that they contain secretions necessary for the harmony of every bodily function.

Healing and Regeneration through Color

The New Age preventive against epidemics, which will replace the present barbaric custom of vaccination, will be the scientific use of color. Each ductless gland, for example, possesses what we may call a "color power" which is the energy radiation visible to extended etheric vision. When properly focused this color power will overcome and eradicate certain diseases caused by a lack of stimulus native to that color.

The color radiation of the pineal gland is blue-lavender; the pituitary, electric blue; the thyroid, green-gold; the solar plexus, orange; the thymus, golden-pink; the adrenals, bright purplish red.

Concentration upon the specific color needed will stimulate the secretion of the gland corresponding to the color, and the flow will aid those parts of the body affected. When the color flow is sufficiently powerful, the body will become immune to the particular malady under consideration. In the care of children and patients too ill to do their own mental work, practitioners skilled in the methods of color-healing will be employed. The ductless glands being concretions of the etheric body, are particularly amenable to the power of thought and color visualization.

Below is a brief tabulation of the general maladies coming under each of the twelve signs:

Aries—Ailments affecting the cerebral hemisphere of the brain, organs of the head, eyes and ears.
Taurus—Neck, throat, larynx, tonsils, carotid arteries and jugular veins.
Gemini—Shoulders, arms, lungs, thymus and upper ribs.
Cancer—Stomach, diaphragm, lacteas and thoracic duct.
Leo—Heart, spinal chord and aorta.
Virgo—Large and small intestines and pancreas.
Libra—Kidneys, skin and the suprarenals.
Scorpio—Bladder, urethra, the genital organs, rectum and descending colon.
Sagittarius—Hips, thighs, femur, illium, illiac arteries and veins and sacral region (lower part of spine).
Capricorn—Knees, bones (in general) and certain skin eruptions.
Aquarius—Limbs from knees to ankles and varicose veins.
Pisces—Maladies, principally of the feet and toes.

It should be noted that indispositions coming under a certain sign may have a reflex in its opposite or complementary sign. This important factor must not be overlooked in making a general diagnosis.

To recapitulate briefly, a complete delineation of a person's conditions of health or disease requires a proper examination of all the numerous factors involved in the whole of his composite being.

All color treatments, when used in conjunction with the harmonious aspects by transit of their corresponding planets, will produce quicker and more lasting effects, particularly if the individual horoscope is also taken into consideration. Lunations and eclipses should always be consulted.

It is interesting to notice that many of the drugs prescribed by the medical profession for certain ailments possess the same vibrations as the colors used in the same cases. A few familiar instances are:

Iron	Red	Aries and Mars
Opium	Violet	Neptune
Cathartics	Electric Blue	Uranus
Astringents	Indigo	Saturn
Disinfectants	Violet Yellow	Mercury

The early healer was, by necessity, both priest and physician. He had great ability in reading and understanding the starry script and a practical knowledge of alchemy, that science which contains the soul signature of herbs in relation to color, fragrance and healing properties. These combined qualifications made the healer truly a wonder worker, a magician among men.

This little treatise is but an humble beginning toward a restoration of the long-lost art of color therapeutics. It will be amplified by many investigators and practitioners until the mystic lore of the past, combined with the scientific discoveries of the present, will reintroduce the priest-physician with true healing power in hand and heart.

Colors operate upon the patient in a threefold manner, physical, mental and spiritual. They may produce a soothing, healing or stimulating effect as occasion or necessity requires. The following colors are suggested for this threefold use:

	Physical	Mental	Spiritual
Soothing:	Misty-gray-blue	Olive Green	Azure Blue
Healing:	Lavender	Golden Green	Lavender Rose
Stimulating:	Clear Red	Orchid	

NEW AGE COLOR-MUSIC

The workings of natural science are being used by denizens of the invisible worlds to increase and accelerate avenues of communication between inner and outer planes. Among the most interesting and fascinating of these New Age wonders is a recent invention—or rather, spiritual discovery—named the *Auroratone,* the manifestations of which are designated as "painting with light."

It differs from the usual color-organ. Not only does it produce a concert of musical masterpieces in both sound and color, but it creates conditions conducive to looking into "higher" realms than those of form and color, thus enabling one to discern thought forms which animated the creations and inspired the original conceptions of their composers.

We have been teaching for many years, both by the spoken and written word, that the chief purpose of Richard Wagner's celestial music will be discovered only when it is used in healing groups or by esoteric students to awaken and stimulate certain vital spiritual centers in the body. This work is particularly effective during that holy interval between the Christmas and Easter Seasons.

Thought forms around which the *Evening Star* from *Tannhauser* is builded revealed white stars massed around a feminine figure robed in white. With the final notes, the figure and stars merged together into a seemingly infinite silver sea. This becomes doubly significant when we realize that the key lesson of *Tannhauser* is *regeneration through purity.*

The *Lohengrin* Prelude revealed hosts of Angels grouped around an ethereal white cup standing like a luminous, transparent lily. As the celestial music soared into its mighty climax, there appeared a golden Sun filled with Beings of a still higher order: Sun Beings who poured golden rays upon the Angelic Hosts as they stood in adoration, with outstretched and uplifted hands to receive this sparkling, golden, effulgence which they in turn focused upon the lily cup as a love gift to man.

Healing and Regeneration through Color

As *Parsival* holds the Good Friday mystery, so *Lohengrin* contains that of Holy Thursday and the Last Supper.

Through this instrument and other inventions the *real* purpose of these beautiful, holy mysteries of the Church will be revealed—no longer as mere ceremonialisms but as magical images depicting definite steps in the spiritual progress of man.

A part of Debussey's music is to make man aware of the reality of nature spirits and their close relationship to humanity. They are all about us, and we will know of their presence if we have eyes to see and ears to hear. Debussey's music is an aid to this awakening.

This composer's *Le Clair de Lune* reveals these etheric beings of fairy kingdoms engaged in various forms of activity. Salamanders, or fire spirits, are seen resolving themselves into a huge gleaming ball, through which they swirl and dance like hosts of minute incandescent sparks. Sylphs, or air spirits, assume the form of a tenuous, floating Grail Cup from which they pour lovely "airy essences" upon earth sprites. Then the latter fashion themselves into a great golden heart whose modulated beats seem to pronounce a tender, multicolored benediction which rays forth from the hearts of multitudes at prayer. Undines, or water spirits, are seen leaping and floating through softly weaving waterfalls in an endless variety of singing colors that reverberate in vast rhythmic rainbows.

The Auroratone opens the door to further miracles belonging to the coming air-age music. It furthers the work of Scriabin, the magic color musician, and deepens appreciation for "between-world" composers such as Debussey and Ravel. Most important of all is the fact that this instrument, by reason of its new motion picture activity, will touch and influence masses of people with its New Age inspirations; thus it will open up new and ever widening oportunities for the development of new processes of healing and spiritual awakening by means of color and music.

In Beethoven's *Moonlight Sonata,* the massed cosmic forces that play upon the earth become visible as magnificent auric emanations of color. They assume various forms on contacting earth's atmosphere, resembling the more beautiful and constructive thought forms projected into the atmosphere by mankind. Their power and radiance, however, greatly exceed anything that humanity can produce.

The higher auric envelopes of earth are flooded at all times with these supernal radiances. It is from them that high spiritual inspiration is drawn for miraculous healings and noble deeds of courage and valor in times of crisis. This was the source of the "etheric visions" described by Raphael, which he immortalized upon his canvasses. It was there also that Beethoven attuned his consciousness to the music of the spheres and then translated something of their harmonies to the earth-world so that man, upon hearing them, might be lifted a little higher Godward.

Beethoven was the Initiate-musician who described in his glorious symphonies some of the mysteries of nature and the intimate relationship between the earth and those great Beings of light who minister about the throne of God. One can catch something of this glory when listening to a great orchestra's rendition of any of his sublime symphonies.

New Age inventions will make pictured tone poems more meaningful to every attentive listener and spectator. "Visible music" is destined to play an important role in the ministry of the beautiful in our world of tomorrow. Its influence will contribute substantially toward increasing man's sensitivity and receptivity to the higher and finer values of life, thus hastening the dissemination of larger and wider knowledge of the deeper mysteries of God and the infinite provisions He has made for enabling man to enter into a more gracious state here and now.

Perhaps the transcendental beauty of a color-tone concert attains its full climax in the presentation of John Charles Thomas singing *The Lord's Prayer* by Albert Hay Malotte. The opening salutation and Amen benediction were marked by bursts of spectrum colors in their clearest and most translucent shadings. The song in its entirety was dominated by a figure of the Christ hovering in blessing among penitants representing various nationalities of the world, all in their respective postures of prayer. This demonstrates the truth that the Lord's Prayer is rightly termed the Universal Petition.

The familiar Hoffman figure of *Christ in Gethsemane* was chosen as most appropriate to place within the magnificent aura of kaleidoscopic colors formed by Mr. Thomas' singing of the words which climax the Prayer so it was used in the first motion picture film to be produced. The Auroratone has extended its benediction of beauty and service to bring solace and upliftment to both body

Healing and Regeneration through Color

and soul of the men in our fighting forces upon far-flung battlefields throughout the world.

So far it is the most important tangible evidence we possess of physical healing through the combined ministry of music and color, a ministry that will come into full manifestation in the New Age, as long since proclaimed by spiritual scientists. It was not invented for purposes of healing. That it possesses such powers was as much a surprise to the inventor as it was to those who, upon witnessing its color-music productions, found themselves healed as by a miracle. Writes one person who experienced such healing: "I look forward to a future wherein we may have Clinics where illness and distress of body, mind and spirit, may be transmuted into health, bouyancy and happiness by the power of Musical Color Harmony."

Among the many unsolicited communications relative to healings unexpectedly received through mere attendance at a recital, the following may be taken as representative of the truly miraculous service the color organ is capable of performing in the field of therapeutics. The letter reads in part as follows:

Four years ago I was taken ill with severe pains in my left breast, which condition was definitely diagnosed by the doctors as cancer of the left breast. These doctors suggested that I take radium treatments, but as I had heard of many others who had taken such treatments without encouraging results, I did not take them myself.

On this memorable afternoon in question, I sat listening to beautiful music and watching the entrancing colors weave themselves into indescribable patterns. As the color recital continued, I became dimly conscious that something was happening inside my body, particularly in the region of my stomach and my left side. Then, at the presentation of The Lord's Prayer, as sung by John Charles Thomas to the beautiful music written by Albert Hay Mallotte, I suddenly became aware that I was actually a completely healed woman.

I went to the doctors for an examination after this amazing experience, and they were puzzled to find that the cancerous lump which had filled my left breast had entirely disappeared.

This was not the only miracle which took place on that afternoon two years ago. For some time I had been the victim of severe painful spasms of the intestines, and I also suffered from a bad eye condition. Both of these afflictions cleared up at the same time as the cancer. That joyful experience took place two years ago, and I have had no sign of any return of any of the conditions since that time.

I do not even pretend to know just what took place in detail on that outstanding afternoon, while I was under the influence of that wonderful Auroratone presentation of Music in Color. All I know is that I was completely healed of cancer right there immediately, all trace having suddenly disappeared, and that God must have been working in a mysterious way, for I am a happy, healthy, pain-free woman once again.

A concert was given for patients in the Los Angeles County General Hospital with most gratifying results, as the following report indicates:

The large auditorium was cleared of all chairs and the patients were wheeled in. Some of them could not raise their heads and nurses had to put extra pillows under their heads so that they could see the screen which was hung high up near the ceiling. The reaction was tremendous. Many of them cried for happiness and the chorus of "God bless you!" was general. The hospital chaplain reported the following day that all of the patients said they slept soundly and many added that they heard the music and saw the floating colors in their dreams all through the night.

The color-music of this Aquarian instrument is being successfully used by St. Tomas Hospital in London, England, and from there is being sent to all parts of the British Isles. A special film has been sent to St. Anne's Hospital, Juneau, Alaska, and Father Hubbard, "The Glacier Priest," sees "immense possibilities" for its healing service and is carrying its ministry to army hospitals in the Aleutians.

Government psychiatrists are contemplating the production of specially prepared music-color films for use in treatment of men who have not been hurt physically, but whose minds have become affected by strain, explosions, fear of battle experiences, and so on. Much interest has been aroused in this experiment.

Ever increasing are the marvels of the New Aquarian Age. Truly, eye hath not seen nor ear heard the wonders which God hath prepared for those that love Him.

COLOR AND THE REGENERATIVE PROCESS

THE HUMAN AURA

God speaks in terms of tone and color, and man is a god in the making. All the attributes of Deity lie latent within him. As the whiteness of his Virgin Spirit enters into ever fuller manifestation, all the colors of the spectrum become visible in a scintillating oval radiance known as the human aura. In this is revealed the degree of development to which he has attained.

The language of color is definite and distinct. Its signature is unmistakable. Every individual process his own dominant three-fold color scheme which is composed of the *fundamental* color denoting his evolutionary status (the permanent aura); the color of his habitual thought (the prevailing aura); the variable, transitory colors of his animating emotion of the moment (the common aura).

If one is centered in spiritual consciousness, the aura's primary hue will be of an azure tone. Such a person being naturally optimistic, his habitual thought is Jupiterian in quality, shown by a deep purple in the aura. His aspirations, directed toward the spiritual, will bring into being a beautiful sunny yellow. This combination produces one of the most exquisitely lovely of all auras, one which well deserves to be called the "wedding garment" of a guest at the Marriage Feast of Christ.

In contrast to the foregoing, the person who is centered in the accumulationof worldly possessions regardless of the manner in which it is accomplished, will be surrounded by dull dark browns, brown being the fundamental color of acquisitiveness. This will be interspersed with heavy dark green, the habitual emanation of one whose dominant interests revolve around self. The variable aura of a person of this nature is frequently heavy grey, representative of the fear which accompanies a sense of separateness in one who lives for self alone and, therefore, apart from and fearful of others.

The human aura forms a miniature aurora borealis—an electrical display of scintillating colors—ever shifting, ever changing in a vivid array. As one develops spiritually this display of auric splendor increases. It is said that when the Lord Gautama Buddha was in meditation his disciples were able to bathe in his aura at a distance of three miles. This splendor of the illuminated soul is poetically described as the *Gem of the King of Kings,* or the *Gem of Sovereignty.* An ancient legend of India declares that, although the earth brought forth the sapphire, the cat's eye, the topaz, the ruby and the two mystic gems that are the favorite of the sun and the favorite of the moon, the Gem of the King of Kings was chief of all these as "the sheen of that jewel spreads round about for a league on every side." Scholars take this to be a reference to the diamond, but that it typified no earthly diamond is revealed in a story of King Milinda to whom was posed the question, "Suppose that on the disappearance of a sovereign overlord, the mystic Gem of Sovereignty lay concealed in a cleft on the mountain peak, and that on another sovereign overlord arriving at the supreme dignity it should appear to him, would you say, O King, that the gem was produced by him?" "Certainly not, sir," replied the king, "the gem would be in its original condition. But it had received, as it were, a new birth through him."

It is also said that the followers of the Persian Master, Mani, referred to the Christ under the title of *The Great Diamond.* As it is known that Mani traveled in India, he was no doubt referring to the *Gem of the King of Kings.*

By the use of fluorescent screens similar to those obtained for X-ray work, modern science has succeeded in photographing the etheric substance or vital body which surrounds and interpenetrates the physical body. Yet more sensitive instruments will be produced in the future by which the tenuous colors of the inner our soul aura will become visible, and thus vindicate still more completely the findings of what is today the occult or hidden science.

THE PROTECTIVE AURA

The aura encircles the body as a frame surrounds a picture. When a person wishes to protect himself from negative influences of any kind, he can build a mental image in which he encases himself. The aura of one who lives above the plane of the senses carries a protective power of blue. One who is given to rational consideration of any subject, undisturbed by emotional reaction, wears an aura of yellow. Golden orange is a preventive against epidemics. An aura of pure white light is a protection against fear of any kind. Let the building of this protective aura be accompanied by the words, "Be still and know that I am God." In this manner one may make himself immune to all malicious attacks, either mental or physical, provided his own heart is free from malice, hatred or vengefulness.

The following excerpt is taken from an old Rosicrucian book:

The highest and deepest occult teaching is that the White Light must never be used for purpose of attack or personal gain, but may properly be employed by anyone, at any time, to protect himself or herself against adverse outside psychic influences, no matter by whom exerted. This is the armor of the spirit and may well be employed in such a way whenever or wherever the need arises.

COLOR VALUES IN CHARACTER BUILDING

To view colors in the superphysical worlds is to behold an infinite sea formed of shimmering rainbows in an ever-ascending series of clarity and beauty. Here a soul may lave in the harmony and rhythm of its own vibratory color tones.

An intellectual soul finds harmony in the yellow, ranging from the deep sun tones of the purely mental up and on into the opalescent rays of intuition. The person of a kindly sympathetic nature responds to the tender, clear green rays.

The cardinal principle of activity is expressed by the pure red rays. The artisans and workers of the world are motivated by powers manifest in this color. The deep opaque reds are destructive; the clear reds constructive. This fact is noticeable during times of war when red becomes the dominant color in feminine fashions and the arts. People themselves may not be conscious of this fact, yet one versed in color psychology can and does observe the hidden effect upon emotions. This condition affects life in all its aspects.

Events, too, have their interior color notes, and when these are of a universal character and charged with deep significance, they quickly translate themselves through human consciousness into corresponding colors on the outer plane of expression. The constant talk of war in 1939 and its actual outbreak before the end of that year made red the predominant fashion color in wearing apparel. As the war spread in 1940, red gained in popularity. Hats, dresses, coats and handbags were conspicuous in any large assemblage of people. This was in keeping with nature's requirements. Red is the color of strength, courage, initiative and physical action. It is valor's own radiation and was, therefore, the predominant quality needed for the successful prosecution of the war.

As the war progressed something else was needed. The stress and strain of '41, '42, and '43 were tending to break the fighting spirit. Morale builders were the supreme need, and so here too, color

Healing and Regeneration through Color 47

played its indispensible part. The brightest possible hues came to the fore, and the more vivid and brilliant the better. This was, therefore, the season of royal purples, bright fuchsias and rich magentas. These colors were, moreover, expressed in most striking combinations. Some were fairly breath-taking. They served to give tone and vibrancy to the spirit, lifting it above doubt and sorrow, depression and despair. They had the effect of turning the mind's eye to the silver lining; the spirit to the brighter days on the other side of the great trial.

The year 1944 was a pastel year. The brilliant and climactic combination of colors was succeeded by soft, soothing tones of all the exquisite pastels. The need of their healing influence had come. The long drawn-out months of war, the suspense and agony of waiting for news, the heart-break evidenced by numerous signals of a golden star, could no longer bear the stress of vivid colors. Victory on the battle front was already conceded, its fulfillment being only a matter of time. Hence, the need was not for greater incitement to action but for more poise for concluding the conflict and making the peace that was to follow. This was the message of the pastels that were introduced to do their work.

This truth found beautiful and effective expression in the Christmastide decorations for 1944. In some of the most famous of our big city department stores, the decorative motifs for window displays and throughout interiors were not so much in the conventional reds and greens, as in rainbow colorings of the most delicate and exquisite tints. In keeping with this color change, it was significant to note that in at least one important instance the traditional Santa Claus was replaced by silver-misted angels.

Commenting on this fact, the manager of such a store expressed the hope that the innovation in their color schemes would tend to lessen the rush and strain and nerve tension of Christmas shoppers.

With 1945 came the cessation of war and the universal call for One World. The need for the solace and healing of the pastels was still with us so they also remained in the front line of fashion. However, it is beautifully fitting that the prevailing color note centered at this time in a lovely blue, the blue that is described as dusty or ash blue. This is the soft, misty shade of the sky in June. It is the color that belongs to healing, to aspiration, to high idealism and to the dreams of a New Day and a New World.

The year 1946 marked the New World in the making. The atomic bomb sounded the death knell of the Old. The thought in everyone's mind and the words on all lips were to the effect that we have now come to a place where it is to be either one world or none. Mass consciousness was concerned as never before with international relations. Again we find this general trend reflected in the prevailing color modes of the day. To quote from a fashion note: "The spring prints all tell their story. There are Gulliver's Travels, and Chinese influence is strongly marked. One designer features a Chinese blouse with Russian decorations, to be worn with a Spanish sash. This is but another evidence that we dress as we feel and think."

As previously noted, red was the dominant color note in the first years of the war. It was the red of destruction. But red is also the color of initiative and action, and as these are needed for the building of the new world, red still has work to do, and is, therefore, well in evidence. But it now appeared in a combination appropriate to its present role. It was linked with gold. Golden yellow is the cementing color, the binder, the unifier. It is the color reflected by the world's efforts to establish the UNO as a successfully functioning world government. And so a current fashion note said that golden red (tomato) was being shown extensively and bid fair to become extremely popular—yet again an expression of color forces at work beneath the surface of things and that become outwardly manifest in our everyday environment.

It is now for the gold in the hearts of mankind to transmute the red of war and conquest into the golden red of the day star, so that humanity may come to walk in the Light as He is in the Light and have true and lasting fellowship, one with another.

The artistic temperament is most responsive to the delicacy of pink and rose rays; especially does the lover of home and home life in all its finest connotations respond to the pure rose tones.

Richard Wagner, the foremost apostle of New Age music, was conscious of the highly sensitizing and refining influences of color upon both mind and body. He aimed to let no fabric but silk touch his bare body, and the color tones so worn were carefully chosen to harmonize with the spirit of the creative work in which he was engaged. Much of Wagner's music deals with the life and activities of the inner or higher planes. In *Lohengrin* and *Parcifal,* for instance, he transcribes for human ears fragments of celestial symphonies. At such highly inspired moments he needed the sensitizing aid of delicate pastels such as the new orchid, the heavenly blues, the crystalline and pale mauves and golden color tones the angels use as mediums of both motion and music in their higher celestial realms.

The soul that is dedicated to God, that seeks a close communion with Him in service and love, finds rest and comfort in the pure, ethereal blues.

The influence of color is being tested in a novel school in Sydney, Australia, according to a news item carried by the Canadian Press, June 20, 1946. The aim is to put colors into the very lives of the children by having them dress in bright colors, work at colored desks and use colored table napkins. Boarders sleep in beds with brightly colored covers, and for daily rest periods the young children are covered with sheets of their favorite color. Pupils are encouraged to choose their own colors for clothing and it is recognized by the head masters of the school that such choice reveals something of the character of the child's nature and upbringing. All lessons, in every grade, stress color values.

This item is insignificant in indicating how rapidly the forces of the inner worlds are now making their impression upon the objective consciousness of mankind in general. As the physical world is the world of form, so the astral world is the realm of color. More and more the outer is reflecting the inner, as the growing color consciousness indicates.

That the reported "color school" should be an Australian enterprise is also in keeping with advanced racial developments, since this is a cradling ground of the New Race even as is our own America.

The sacrificial one finds peace and harmony in the Christed golden ray, which is more gold than yellow and is more brilliant than the ordinary yellow ray.

The lover of mankind, the one whose life is filled with compassion, is closely attuned to the violet ray. This is the blue of love purified by the red of suffering, for only through love and suffering is compassion born.

It is important to understand more fully the power of color in regard to its effect on life, since only then can consideration be given to its use in the home, school and public buildings of all kinds. The decorative motif should be in harmony with the purpose to which the building is dedicated, whether this be learning, living or worship. In New Age schools the pupils will be instructed in methods of visualizing the colors of physical, mental or spiritual states which are to become permanent attributes.

The Stelp School in Wilmette, Ill., received a new paint job. Walls were in pastel hues; boards, dark green; chalk, yellow. "There's an entirely different attitude now," says Gordon Walker, an instructor. "There's no afternoon let-down. The kids stay awake and always are ready for something."

From the *New York Times,* Nov. 2, 1948:

The effect of schoolroom colors on children was a matter of utmost concern to education officials . . . the formerly prevailing brown scheme, which is said to have a depressing effect on youngsters, is to go . . .

Harold D. Hynds, Supt. of the Bureau of Plant Operation, explained that scientific experiments indicate that color is a factor in molding attitudes and viewpoints of children. Light-colored walls and ceilings, together with sufficient natural or artificial light, will produce an environment which promotes health and is conducive to study.

The Ladies Home Journal published an item about Teachers College, New York. The traditional library was high-ceilinged, shadowed by pillars and panelled in oak with Tudor carvings—like a funeral home. Interior decorators threw tradition out of the window, and now the walls are panelled in yellow, rose and Bermuda tans. The flying buttresses are elm-green, ceilings and cornices similarly brightened, giving the whole the friendly charm of a Dutch kitchen. Result: circulation has zoomed.

Architects, educators and psychologists collaborated on three Baltimore school buildings. The latter saw to it that there was proper lighting, that the "blackboards" were green, the chalk yellow and the walls in delicate tints. Children's lunches are served in vari-colored plastic dishes to give brightness and beauty. Apathetic children were stimulated to new interest in their studies when the walls of another schoolroom were painted in Wedgewood blue, the trim and cloakroom in bright yellow. The blackboards are no longer black but cream-colored and written on with royal-blue chalk.

According to Dr. William Jansen, a Supt. of Schools, vandalism has decreased where schools are attractively painted. He declared that the "entire tone of a community can be raised by the children's awareness of the beauty and cheerfulness of color."

In a lecture given recently by a prominent modernistic architect, the New Age residence was described as being mostly white on its exterior and as having three sides of every room open to light. The twelve zodiacal colors are called into service in interior motifs. A design was shown in which the rooms were grouped around a large central dining salon with a dome-like arrangement. From the top of this dome a camera obscura reflected surrounding scenery upon walls of the dining room in a continuous series of motion pictures.

From Dallas, Texas, come the ideas of Carl Smedley, a color expert for a paint concern, on letting color solve human problems. "Now take the case of a cantankerous business executive who came to our office.... When the walls of his office were changed from an off-yellow color to a two-tone green, his disposition became as gentle as a lamb's." He told of one lady who had a putty-colored kitchen. When painters substituted canary yellow above, white below, and delphinium blue in nook and for ceiling, she wrote that her husband's early morning grouch entirely disappeared.

Light, color and beauty are to be key-words to New Age living. The Aquarian Age is essentially and primarily a color age. Lighter or higher color tones of the spectrum are coming into visibility as, on the one hand, the atmosphere becomes clearer and more attenuated and the ethers more discernible; and, on the other hand, man's sense perception becomes more highly sensitized. With such changes in man and his environment we may expect to lay hold of hitherto undreamed of powers linked to color radiations. New and amazing developments in the psychology and therapeutics of color are nearing practical application and public use.

A manual was prepared on color for printers, publishers and advertisers by The National Research Bureau, Inc., Chicago. The work is stated to be the result of twenty-five years of research in color values and is entitled *The Color Prophet*. This is no simple restatement of familiar principles in general, but an exhaustive scientific treatise on the subject such as one would have reason to expect in a work that sells, not for a few cents or even a dollar or two but for the very substantial price of $35.00. It is further evidence of our growing color consciousness. The manual contains an analysis of the following major aspects of each color: psychological effect; symbolic meaning; legibility value; visibility and attention power; identity and retention power; appropriate use.

A hundred years ago newspapers were packed tight with small type print. There were no light spaces, no spread-eagle headlines, no pictures and no color. Now we have all these, though colors in the dailies have not yet gone beyond the "funnies" or certain tinted pages. But we have color photography, technicolor films and many magazines with colored illustrations in profusion. It will probably not be long before the morning paper will come in colors to pep the reader up for the day, and the evening paper in tones designed to prepare him for a comfortable armchair and a night's sound sleep.

New York's new subway cars are coming in color. The exteriors are done in a two-tone gray with orange striping, and the interiors are decorated in a bright blue-and-gray color scheme, lighted by rows of fluorescent fixtures. Seats are upholstered in striped plastic and the floors have been dressed up by a resilient blue-gray covering with yellow markings.

Yes, and a California beekeeper has invented a process by which he is producing honey in six different colors.

It is well to be surrounded by the color to which one's soul responds or for which one feels a need in his development. Regardless of outside environment, the soul can always touch color vibration by lifting itself in communion and prayer. Bathing in the golden radiance of the Christ Light or submerging oneself in azure harmonies are not mere poetic fancies. They are glorious and divine techniques for acquiring power, understanding and beauty. They serve to further spiritual growth and to assist in the rehabilitation of the individual—and thus, of the world.

The following list is given as representative of the psychological effects produced by the powers of color.

1. Clear blue—A high degree of spirituality.
2. Blue, tinged with lavender—High idealism.
3. Blue, mixed with dark reddish brown—Selfish religious feeling.

4. Blue, mixed with grey—Religious feeling, tinged with fear.
5. Blue, mixed with black—Religious feeling, tinged with superstition.
6. Lavender—High degree of spirituality.
7. Violet—Complete spiritual dedication.
8. Orchid—The illumined clairvoyant.
9. Lilac—Altruism.
10. Pure yellow—Spiritualized intellect.
11. Orange—Intellect predominant.
12. Orange mixed with brick red—Low type of mental cunning.
13. Light clear green—Sympathy, understanding; the magic color used by fairies.
14. Green, medium—Adaptability.
15. Green, medium, tinged with reddish brown and flecked with with dark red or reddish black—Jealousy.
16. Green and grey, mingled—Deceit.
17. Pure carmine—Pure human affection.
18. Scarlet—Self pride or self will.
19. Bright brick red—Anger.
20. Deep red, mingled with brown—Sensuality.
21. Rose, pure—Unselfish and constant affection.
22. Old Rose mixed with reddish brown—Selfish affection.
23. Brown—Acquisitiveness.
24. Reddish brown—Avarice.
25. Greenish and reddish brown—Selfishness.
26. Dark grey mixed with brown and red—Depression.
27. Livid pale grey—Fear.
28. Black—Secretive; occult. All things in latency. Considered unfortunate because few have sufficient understanding to use these vast hidden powers.

SUPERNATURAL POWERS IN COLOR

The prismatic spectrum is a vast storehouse of supernatural forces. At present little of this power is known or even suspected by the average layman and still less by the scientist.

Red, intoning base etheric notes, is the color of fire. It is through these notes that a human being has his first approach to Deity. In most of the world religions God is represented as appearing in flames of fire. From this came worship of the fire that is never extinguished, with its vestal priestesses and its votive offerings.

Red fire is only one phase of God in manifestation. His power is infinite; its expression an ever ascending spiral of color and tone. This is evidenced again in hymnal worship ascribed to the seven vowels as power ciphers of the Seven Angels of the Planets. This power is disseminated by means of the sevenfold scale in both color and tone. In its ascending rhythms, the red of terrestial fire is transmuted into the golden yellow of pure spirit essence. By use of its magical golden color, miracles of healing and transformation can be performed. A portion of this magic has been condensed into that most perfect of all metals, the sun's high gift to this planet, gold.

Gold was held sacred by primitive peoples, who were wiser in esoteric truths than we moderns. Its use was never permitted to become common, but was reserved for temple worship. The misuse of gold has brought destruction instead of strength and elevaton. Man has forfeited the rights of its blessings and is fast losing the use of the metal as well, for its prostitution has brought upon him a heavy karmic debt which involves our entire planet.

Green is the nature color. It belongs to summer and the Moon, and is known as the Mother of Nature. In the radiations of this magic light fairies perform their enchantments over field and forest. In countries where many peoples possess "second sight" and hold communion with the "little people of nature," green is held in high esteem, even to the point of veneration in some instances. Ireland is a notable example of this fact.

Blue describes the sea and sky, symbols of infinity for humanity. It frees man from "the prison house of flesh" and lifts him above all physical limitations, carrying him into Elysian fields where he may drink of the waters of life. Blue reaches into infinity, so that the soul may know that Love and Immortality and God are one.

As night brings a recapitulation of the day, and as death serves to assemble all the events of the past life into conscious totality, so does the indigo ray receive and unify the forces of all the prismatic colors into one great force. Its keynote is Universality—God in man and man in God. The human consciousness must be raised to this realization before the higher, freer color rays can be released upon the planet; or in other words, before a new spectrum can be brought into visibility.

In the purple ray is sounded the exalted soul song of God. Purple, the royal color, is associated with earthly power and splendor. It is the color most prominent in the coronation of kings and High Priests. Purple indicates that the lower red fire of sense life has been lifted into the pure blue of spiritual life.

Jupiter, to whom the purple ray is ascribed, is ever associated with the sacred rites of fire. Its keynote is transmutation.

Black is a Saturnian color, and Saturn is the home of all beginnings. In order to symbolize the hidden, secretive phase of their work, many Temples of Initiation are draped in black. Black is similarly used in Masonic Rites. In religious art, the Madonna and Babe are sometimes depicted in black, thus signifying the mysteries of the Incarnation. The highest truths are discoverable only by those who have the courage to pass beyond all sight and sound into the Great Darkness that precedes the Light of Eternal Day.

White, the opposite pole of black, contains the active manifestation of all life. The white piano keys are outpouring; the black keys enfolding. White is the light and action of day; black the darkness and silence of night. White is dynamic and stimulating; black is mysterous and inspiring. White is revelation: black is concealment.

White, embracing all colors, is the Cosmic Day. Black, enfolding all colors, is the Cosmic Night. When their sublime forces blend, the perfect Aeonic Cycle is complete.

COLOR AND THE FOUR SACRED SEASONS

Each of the four sacred seasons sounds its own particular keynote and emanates its own special color. The color of the Autumn Equinox is a soft and exquisite blue like the mist which veils mountain tops in early dawn. Blue is a color of tremendous power. It is the Father color.

The color of the Winter Solstice, the birth color, is a luminous white. The highest ecstatic impulses always find expression in white. And it is in the divine pulsations of white light that the Hosts of heaven chorus of the coming to earth of the Holy Child.

The color of the Spring Equinox is the beautiful red of new life, the beginnings of a new vibrancy which pulses throughout the planet at the time of the spiritual New Year.

The color of the Summer Solstice is a luminous gold, the Lord Christ's own color, for the Summer Solstice is His particular season when He ascends in glory to the very throne of God the Father and bathes in the divine ecstasy of a perfect at-onement with Him.

The four principal steps in human birth have their parallel in the four great planetary cycles. Man in his increasing materialism has forgotten the true significance of these successive stages of development. The first step of the Birth Ritual is that of the Annunciation and corresponds to the high golden ecstasy of the season of the Summer Solstice. As the sun passes into Virgo, the Christ turns His powerful golden inflow towards the earth. The celestial hosts of Virgo are the foci for his downpouring force. As this new Christed light floods through the etheric sheaths of the planet, all the plant kingdom becomes luminous. September is the most fitting time in which to hold high communion with Nature. In the reverent and awe-inspiring sacred hush of this season the earth experiences the wonder of the planetary Immaculate Conception.

At the holy time of the Autumn Equinox the golden Christ Ray blends with the blue, and the atmosphere is suffused with a rare shimmering blue-gold. Now it is that the Celestial Hosts of Libra join in heavenly hallelujahs, for the Christ force touches the outermost edge of earth's physical envelope, the sacred moment of the quickening occurs. All the planet is imbued with a new life impulse, and its vibratory rhythms are lifted.

From the Autumn Equinox until the Winter Solstice every day is a Holy Day in which dedicated ones may walk increasingly in the Light. For each day of this sacred interval the golden Christ Light penetrates deeper into the earth until, at the Winter Solstice (December twenty-first), it is focussed in the very heart of the earth, as jubilant Hosts chant of the midnight birth of a new Sun.

Thus we see that our earth planet becomes a beautiful rainbow of color, and also a sublime symphony of sound. Two of the sacred seasons, the Spring Equinox and the Summer Solstice, ray forth colors which are brilliant and vivid, attuned to the majestic tones of a major symphony. The other two sacred seasons ray forth colors which are soft and luminous, attuned to the tender tones of a minor symphony. Thus we come to note something of our planetary rhythms of light and shadow. And by shadow we mean the softened, muted, minor tones.

All mankind lives unconsciously in harmony with these alternating seasons. In Spring and Summer man seeks the open and pursues interests belonging to objective life. In Autumn and Winter he turns to inner and more serious things belonging to subjective life. Our educational system follows this pattern: relaxation in Spring and Summer; application to study in Autumn and Winter.

The Autumn Equinox is the time for deepening soul dedication, for renewal of soul aspiration. It is a time to tune in with the inner processes of nature and to conform the activities of the inner life to the spiritual character of the season. In this way the disciple will come into a personal realization of the harmony that exists between the life and character of the Lord Christ and all other world Teachers with that of nature, which is God in manifestation. Thus does he take on some of these same qualities and join the ranks of that ever growing number of men and women whose uppermost purpose is to assist the Christ in his redemptive work for humanity and to advance His reign on earth.

SPIRITUAL SIGNIFICANCE OF THE SPECTRUM

I do set my bow in the cloud, and it shall be for a token of a covenant between me and the earth.
—*Gen. 9:13*

It is only as one begins to comprehend something of the profound import of color that the deeper significance of the above words are revealed.

It must first be understood that the color-tones have passes and are passing through a process of evolution which is in complete harmony with the evolution of mankind. Our earliest humanity did not see the present seven-color spectrum any more than our average present-day man can see the twelve-color spectrum that will be visible to a more highly evolved race in future ages.

Primitive man recognized none of the colors that we know today. He was able to distinguish only the difference between light and dark, or black and white. God's first mantram, "Let there be light," concealed rather than revealed the seven physical colors with which we are now familiar.

During the Atlantean civilization red, orange and green were perceptible, also deeper shades of blue, but man as yet had no conception of those exquisite color-tones we call azure and mauve. The blue sky as observed by the ancients was a deep, dark tone far different from the dazzling azure of our June days, of which the poet sang,

What is so rare as a day in June?
Then if ever come perfect days.

The rainbow, with its seven color rays, is a cosmic proclamation of the divinity of man. It reveals that a stage of evolution has been attained wherein the human life wave has evolved a sevenfold body; and the Ego, now fully awake, dominant and triumphant,

Healing and Regeneration through Color

possesses and controls this wonderful sevenfold vehicle. The Divine within canticles seven cosmic tones that descend to earth in the seven notes of our diatonic scale. It bathes in seven-rayed color waves, whereby the hitherto dormant seven jewels of the sevenfold body are being aroused. This quickening by means of color and tone proclaim the findings of the kingdom of heaven within, with all of its manifold and illimitable prerogatives.

This is the spiritual message of the rainbow.

Red, the first color-note of the spectrum, is the note of activity, challenge, adventure. It is here that the mass consciousness of mankind is centered. Red is the dominant decorative motif of most primitive peoples. Its emanation is physically stimulating. This ray is used for melancholia, anemia, all forms of sluggishness, retardation of blood circulation. Surrounding oneself with red is a splendid antidote for fear and timidity.

Excess of activity is a sign of danger. Hence, red lights are used as traffic stop signals. Mephistopheles and Satan are always symbolized by the color red because excessive activity in any direction leads to negative reactions which we term sins—the work of the evil one. The transmutation of deep, dark crimson tones within the human aura into the clear, bright red of bravery, courage and daring is one of the most important steps in human evolution.

Orange, the next higher ray of the spectrum, is produced by blending two primary colors, red and yellow. Red, as previously noted, is the activity ray. Yellow is the mental or wisdom ray. Orange, therefore, is a color of tremendously dynamic power for healing. Visualizing the orange ray as encircling and permeating afflicted parts often brings instant relief. This is the ray of discrimination, the capacity for making wise decisions.

Yellow, a primary, has been termed the mind color, and it proves itself to be a vibrant and refreshing mental stimulant. Its vibratory rate is high, its influence elevating and inspiring. The halo around the heads of saints is always depicted in golden yellow. It is generally recognized as the color-note of the Christ and the Illuminati, for it sings of infinity rather than concreteness. It lifts above the mundane. It soars up and away, reaching ever toward the supreme goal which is Light. To become one with the yellow ray is to comprehend the unreality of matter and the eternalness of Spirit. This is the true meaning of Wisdom.

Green is a secondary color, produced by combining yellow with blue. The blue ray is a force direct from Spirit. The yellow ray is wisdom or soul power. Thus, green represents a commingling of soul with Spirit. Man must fashion his soul during his evolutionary progress, but Spirit is God, eternal and immortal. Green is the color associated with life; and the primary purpose of life is to build a soul and to unite it with Spirit.

Green is the color of earth. Each resurrection season nature adorns herself in robes of shining green. Forests radiate such powerful and magnetic life emanations that highly sensitized persons are not only renewed but can actually see them. Everyone knows the sense of rest, well being and refreshment gained from a prolonged stay amidst the greens of nature. This is the ray most efficacious for soothing tired or frayed nerves, for headache and other upsets caused by nerve tension.

Blue, as we have said, is the Spirit ray. Deep, dark blue indicates power of tremendous intensity. Light or azure tones imply high and etherial aspirations. This is the ray in which creative artists should immerse themselves before beginning work. Dr. Babbitt, father of color-healing, states that he used the blue ray in all forms of inflammation and various diseases of the skin.

When on visualizes blue, the head instinctively lifts, the eyes raise, for blue is the color of the sky, of mountain crests at dawn and sunset, of smoke as it spirals upward from chimney tops. Blue lifts, exalts and inspires one toward ever greater heights of endeavor and attainment.

Green reaches outward, blue lifts upward. Therefore, we may say that green is a horizontal color while blue is a vertical color. Together they form the cross which is the symbol of life.

Indigo is the summation or infolding, as it were, of all colors. This is the ray of introspection. It is, perhaps, the most difficult of all colors to visualize accurately; but if, through persistent effort, one becomes adept at this visualization, doors of the subconscious will be unbarred and long buried soul memories will be restored—for indigo is the color-bridge between the finite and the Infinite. Its keynote is univerality. It is the expression of God concealed in Mary, of man enfolded in God. The indigo ray may be used to advantage in deep scientific and philosophic research.

Violet (purple) is the transmutation color. As transmutation is

Healing and Regeneration through Color

concerned with the most advanced phases of spiritual development, so violet is the highest color vibration of the spectrum. It is the seventh color ray, and seven is the number denoting transmutaton: four (matter) plus three (Spirit). Their blending attains the supreme goal of human evolution; hence, seven is the principal number of the earth planet.

Violet is also a secondary color, formed by blending red (matter) with blue (Spirit). The process of transforming lower man into higher is always accompanied by much travail, so the darker tone (purple) has become associated with pain and sorrow. When the transforming process is complete one becomes a king and the son of the Great King. "Royal purple" and "born to the purple" are expressions of deep spiritual significance. Wagner immersed himself in this ray when he was ready to transcribe the music of angels for his transcendent operas.

To lift, to ennoble, to spiritualize all life is the message of the color scale, the high significance of the spectrum and of the gleaming bow set in the cloud.

BLACK AND WHITE

Black is the feminine complement of white. White is active, black is passive. White is positive, black is negative. White is all-revealing, black is all-concealing.

Black is another designation for Chaos, the seed-ground of Infinity; the seed-ground of the unmanifest, the uncharted. Visualizing intense blackness stimulates latent and hitherto undeveloped soul faculties. When from the celestial core of this blackness a point of white light emerges, without solicitation or premeditation, finer and higher forces are awakening within. Into the utter blackness of Chaos, God sent His supreme mandate. Light was born. As the divinity in man comes into fuller expression, the white light flames forth. Man becomes divine when black and white have merged. Then human evolution is at an end.

In his *Theory of Color,* Goethe, one of the world's most profound mystics, gave to man a textbook on this subject which will be a classic in the incoming New Age. To him color was the Voice of God speaking through nature. Blackness was not merely an absence of light; it was the background of the cosmos, a field of intense activity for Beings of a vastly higher order than our humanity.

Azure-white light is the highest concept of man. It entirely transcends physical vision, so "seeing" it must be always a spiritual experience. The light has been used since time immemorial by Wise Men, the Illuminati, as a means of both physical and mental protection for their disciples. There are recorded thousands of instances when miraculous protection was given by surrounding an individual with an aura of white light in times of great emergency.

One occasion of special interest has to do with a hospital located several miles distant from Hiroshima. When the atomic bomb struck, no one was seriously injured, although many persons were knocked down and suffered minor bruises and cuts. The amazing factor was that no person dressed all in white received any kind of hurt despite the fact that many so clothed were working in close proximity to the injured.

White light is weighted with the power to bless. It is God speaking through the manifold activities of creation. When man learns to tune in and freely utilize this transcendent force, many limitations and disabilities of this three-dimensional world will be conquered or eliminated. Then will man assume his rightful place as an "heir and joint heir with Christ," a true son of God in full possession of his divine heritage.

CONCLUSION

So it is that all experiences of life may be deciphered in terms of color. As the most ethereal and exquisite of all English poets sings, "Life is a dome of many colored glass staining the white radiance of eternity."

God is Light. The more intimate our color experiences become, the closer our attunement with God, the All-good. It is possible to live so intimately with a color that it becomes a part of oneself. Then its soul secrets are revealed, its inner force laid bare. The entranced observer suddenly comprehends a deeper significance to the pink flush of dawn or the shadows of purple twilight. In a vast new miracle of revelation color will become audible as well as visible, and all nature resonant with proclamations of glory. It was surely after such a subliminal experience that Goethe declared, "Nature conceals God, but not from everyone." In the exaltation of this high consciousness one learns to "walk in the light as he is in the light"—a glorious forecast from pioneers of the New Day.

Communion with the soul of color lifts one beyond realms of matter, up into spheres of spirit, on and away into cosmic space, for Light is universal, infinite.

Every cosmic truth finds its reflection in man. Humanity, too, functions in harmony (more or less) with the threefold principle found in the primaries—red, blue and yellow. He *thinks* in yellow. He *feels* in red. He *wills* in blue.

Goethe concludes his *Theory of Color* with these most significant and revealing words: "When we have first grasped this parting from one another of yellow and blue, and especially their intensification into red, and in observing them for a long time have seen how these opposites incline toward each other and are united in the third, then it is certain that a deep secret will begin to dawn upon us that a spiritual meaning may underlie these two separate and opposite beings. And we shall scarcely be able to hold ourselves back from acknowledging that when we see them bringing forth here below, the green is there above the red that we are beholding; on one side the earthly, and on the other side the heavenly creations of the Elohim."

— FINIS —